MOMENTS WITH ONESELF SERIES: 6

PROBLEM IS YOU
SOLUTION IS YOU

SWAMI DAYANANDA SARASWATI

ARSHA VIDYA

ARSHA VIDYA
RESEARCH AND PUBLICATION TRUST
CHENNAI

Published by :

Arsha Vidya Research and Publication Trust
4 ' Sri Nidhi ' Apts 3rd Floor
Sir Desika Road Mylapore
Chennai 600 004 INDIA
Tel   : 044 2499 7023
Telefax : 2499 7131
Email   : avrandpt@gmail.com
Website: www.avrpt.com

ISBN : 978-81-904203-1-0

Revised Edition	: August	2007	Copies : 2000
1st Reprint	: May	2009	Copies : 2000
2nd Reprint	: November	2009	Copies : 2000
3rd Reprint	: May	2012	Copies : 1000

Design & Layout :
Graaphic Design

Printed at :
Sudarsan Graphics
27, Neelakanta Mehta Street
T. Nagar, Chennai 600 017
Email : info@sudarsan.com

CONTENTS

KEY TO TRANSLITERATION AND PRONUNCIATION OF
SANSKRIT LETTERS

Sanskrit is a highly phonetic language and hence accuracy in articulation of the letters is important. For those unfamiliar with the *Devanāgari* script, the international transliteration is a guide to the proper pronunciation of Sanskrit letters.

अ	*a*	(b*u*t)		ट	*ṭa*	(*t*rue)*3
आ	*ā*	(f*a*ther)		ठ	*ṭha*	(an*th*ill)*3
इ	*i*	(*i*t)		ड	*ḍa*	(*d*rum)*3
ई	*ī*	(b*ea*t)		ढ	*ḍha*	(go*dh*ead)*3
उ	*u*	(f*u*ll)		ण	*ṇa*	(u*n*der)*3
ऊ	*ū*	(p*oo*l)		त	*ta*	(pa*th*)*4
ऋ	*ṛ*	(*rh*ythm)		थ	*tha*	(*th*under)*4
ॠ	*ṝ*	(ma*ri*ne)		द	*da*	(*th*at)*4
ऌ	*ḷ*	(reve*lry*)		ध	*dha*	(brea*the*)*4
ए	*e*	(pl*ay*)		न	*na*	(*n*ut)*4
ऐ	*ai*	(*ai*sle)		प	*pa*	(*p*ut) 5
ओ	*o*	(g*o*)		फ	*pha*	(loo*ph*ole)*5
औ	*au*	(l*ou*d)		ब	*ba*	(*b*in) 5
क	*ka*	(see*k*) 1		भ	*bha*	(a*bh*or)*5
ख	*kha*	(bloc*kh*ead)*1		म	*ma*	(*m*uch) 5
ग	*ga*	(*g*et) 1		य	*ya*	(lo*ya*l)
घ	*gha*	(lo*g h*ut)*1		र	*ra*	(*r*ed)
ङ	*ṅa*	(si*ng*) 1		ल	*la*	(*l*uck)
च	*ca*	(*ch*unk) 2		व	*va*	(*va*se)
छ	*cha*	(cat*ch h*im)*2		श	*śa*	(*s*ure)
ज	*ja*	(*j*ump) 2		ष	*ṣa*	(*sh*un)
झ	*jha*	(he*dg*ehog)*2		स	*sa*	(*s*o)
ञ	*ña*	(bu*n*ch) 2		ह	*ha*	(*h*um)

•	ṁ	*anusvāra*	(nasalisation of preceding vowel)
:	ḥ	*visarga*	(aspiration of preceding vowel)
*			No exact English equivalents for these letters

1.	Guttural	–	Pronounced from throat
2.	Palatal	–	Pronounced from palate
3.	Lingual	–	Pronounced from cerebrum
4.	Dental	–	Pronounced from teeth
5.	Labial	–	Pronounced from lips

The 5th letter of each of the above class – called nasals – are also pronounced nasally.

TWO TYPES OF PROBLEMS

There are two types of problems in life; one is a problem for which the solution lies outside the problem; the other is a problem for which the solution is within the very problem.

The problems of food, clothing, shelter and so on, belong to the first category; you need to seek solution outside. Let us take the problem of hunger. You need food to appease your hunger. The solution, food, lies outside the problem, hunger. If you do not have shelter, you have to get one, since it is not available with you; it is outside you. Therefore, you seek the solution in an external situation. There are many such problems in your individual life, social life, and in your national life. These may be called situational problems. Taking into account the resources at your disposal, planning and effort, you can solve them.

Let us suppose that someone gives you a jigsaw puzzle involving few pieces, and when arranged in a particular manner, form the word 'YES'. Each piece has its own shape and angularity. Individually they do not make any sense. They become meaningful only when arranged in a given manner. However, when you juggle with these pieces, trying different arrangements, they do not form the word 'YES'. When you are not able to solve the puzzle inspite of repeated attempts, and you are not able to see the pieces falling in their place, you may construe that a piece is missing. You may think that the solution lies outside the problem, outside the ten pieces; maybe a eleventh or even a twelfth piece is necessary to solve the puzzle. It is not so. The ten pieces alone are required. It is the second kind of problem where the solution lies within the problem. To solve this kind of a problem requires an informed, enlightened person who knows the solution. The person has the solution in his or her head and can see the word 'YES' within the ten pieces even when they are not assembled. The *āpta*, the enlightened person, has to tell you that the solution is within the problem and that you have to arrange the pieces in a particular manner to arrive at the solution. We shall be talking about the second kind of problem, where the solution is within the problem.

If the solution is contained in the problem and yet remains a problem, it is purely due to ignorance. The problem is caused by ignorance of a fact. The knowledge of the fact alone solves the problem.

PROBLEM OF HUMAN SADNESS

Problem of human sadness has the solution within itself. Generally, you think the solution to this problem of sadness lies outside because you always find reasons external to yourself. It appears that there is a factor other than you that causes sadness. That factor needs to be corrected, mended, amended or even destroyed to remove your sadness. It is easy enough to find a reason for sadness. If you ask someone, "Why are you sad?" he or she will have various reasons such as, "I am sad because I do not have a job; because I am ill; because I am not married yet; because I am married; because I do not have children; because I have too many of them; because someone has not written; because someone has written." The ingenuity of the human mind is able to discover causes for sorrow outside itself. The conclusion is, sorrow or sadness is a problem whose solution lies outside.

Let us examine whether a solution can come from outside. If you conclude you are sad because you do not have a job, it implies that your sadness should completely disappear when you get a job. It should be able to make you free from sadness. But when you do get a job, you find you have a new problem; perhaps, the place of work is too far away. You have to spend half your time travelling, going to the bus stop, waiting for the bus, travelling by bus for one hour, and again walking to the factory. It would be much more convenient if your house was close to the factory. You look for a house nearby and when you get one, you discover another problem. The air is polluted since it is an industrial area. How can anyone live there? The old house was definitely better and you return to the old place; but then, it is also a return to the old problem of distance and commuting. You solve one problem and another one crops up in its place. The problems of job, transportation, and accommodation are situations and cannot really be the cause of sadness.

If you think a given situation is a source of sadness, you will find it is also a source of comfort. Your mother-in-law is always a source of sorrow but when you want to go to a movie or listen to a Swami, you prefer to leave your child at home. The mother-in-law becomes very handy as a baby-sitter. So, even a mother-in-law can be a source of comfort. Any given thing that you look upon as a problem also offers you advantages and vice versa. Nothing in the creation is one-sided. You examine anything or any situation. If you become a Swami there is an advantage when you are amidst people; people spare you from certain questions at least. But then you are bothered by other kinds of questions: "Swamiji, do you read palms? Can you tell me when will I get married?" Long ago, when I visited a famous zoo in Milwaukee, United States, I heard a youngster saying to another, "Hey, look at this new one!" So, being a *sādhu* also has its advantages and disadvantages. If you get married, there are advantages and some disadvantages too. If you do not get married, there are many advantages but some disadvantages also. Having children gives a sense of fulfilment but bringing them up has its own problems. If you examine any situation, you will find both advantages and disadvantages. it means if a situation can cause you sadness, then that very situation can also be a source of comfort. If you are comfortable because of a situation, you can also become sad because of a situation.

CAN POSITIVE THINKING REMOVE SADNESS?

You can look at anything in more than one way. You can look at a rose and remark, "Oh, the rose is beautiful but it has thorns," or "In spite of thorns, the rose is beautiful." Both views are all right, because they are based on facts. This reminds me of the so-called 'positive thinking' that people talk about these days. It is a way of looking at things. "Rose is beautiful, but it has thorns," is the complaining way of looking at a rose. "In spite of thorns, the rose is beautiful," is a positive way of looking at it. There are many people who advocate positive thinking as a means to overcome sadness. However, it cannot solve the problem of human sadness for good, for where there is positive thinking there must be a fact that makes it a factual positive thinking. If it is so, there is going to be another fact forming the basis for negative thinking.

Take the case of a man with a poor self-image. He felt he had not made his life, he was a failure. He looked down upon himself. People around him also confirmed his opinion of himself. Nobody could really help him out of it. He went to a Swami to seek help. The Swami told him, "Look at yourself positively. Look at all the things that you have. You have a pair of eyes that sees properly, a pair of ears that hears properly. There are so many people who have no eyes and many others who are deaf. You have all the senses intact, a healthy body, and a good mind. How many people are there who are so privileged as you? You have good education and good parentage.

There are so many orphans who do not even know their parents and countless others who have no education at all. You also have a nice family, a good job and a comfortable house. Really speaking, you are blessed. Why do you have such low image of yourself? You have so many positive things about yourself." When the Swami reassured him, the man was convinced, "Yes, there is really nothing to complain about. I am quite happy now. Thank you, Swami." The man happily walked out.

As the man was leaving, he saw someone stepping out of a Mercedes. Equipped with positive thinking, he looked at the person. He noticed that this man also had a pair of eyes, a pair of ears, a healthy body, and he had a Mercedes! This man had everything plus a Mercedes while he did not even have a scooter. All his positive thinking evaporated. Positive thinking does not work. It is silly. If positive thinking is based on facts, so is negative thinking. It is a fact that both of them had all the advantages, but one man had the car while the other did not.

As long as there are facts, negative thinking will always exist along with positive thinking. The conclusion, "I am sad," will ever remain with you because you think sadness is caused by the external world. Positive thinking cannot erase the conclusion, "I am sad."

CAN CHANGE IN SITUATION REMOVE SADNESS?

If external world is the cause for your sadness, you cannot get rid of it by creating a new situation or going to a new place. Even if you go to heaven, the most perfect of places, your sadness will remain. Let us see how.

There are different concepts of heaven. According to our scriptures, there is no hunger or thirst, no old age or death in heaven. All you have in heaven is dance and music. You will get bored.

According to a religious sect in the West, the faithful will go to heaven and have eternal dinner with God. A typical Western dinner starts with soup, so the eternal dinner will also start with soup. Since it is eternal, you will be seated at the table, eternally. You cannot take even one sip of soup because if the dinner begins, it also has to end. You will have to keep the spoon with soup near your mouth but not taste the soup. You cannot continue and you are stuck with soup.

Further in heaven, the residents have varying status and, therefore, experience different degrees of joy, since the status can give happiness. Our scriptures give a detailed description of the degree of happiness associated with each status.

Imagine a young man who is strong, healthy, brave and has clear thinking. He is well brought-up, well educated, leads a life of *dharma* and so has no conflicts in his mind. He owns the entire earth with all its resources, with neither a rival nor another to demand a share or threaten. All these will obviously give him the highest degree of happiness that a human being can ever hope to enjoy. Let us call it one unit of happiness. Multiply it by one hundred and you get one unit of happiness enjoyed by *manuṣya-gandharvas*. The happiness enjoyed by *deva-gandharvas* is hundred times that of *manuṣya-gandharvas* and it goes on. Keep multiplying by one hundred each time and you can get an estimate of the degree of happiness enjoyed by the *pitṛs*, the *ājāna-devas*, who are born in heaven, the *karma-devas*, who serve the *devas* such as Indra, Bṛhaspati, Prajāpati, and Brahmā. The idea is different status gives different degrees of joy. So even in heaven, comparisons will make you feel inadequate.

Most of our youngsters' ambition is to go abroad. Their first choice is, of course, the U.S.A, failing which it is Canada. If not that, it is Saudi Arabia, Kuwait, Dubai, or Bahrain. If none of these, well, it is Malaysia, Singapore, Hong Kong... somewhere away from India. This is the ambition of most of the youngsters, although I am sure there are exceptions. This reminds me of an incident. One of my devotee from Kerala was doing well in Kuwait. I had been there for some talks. When I met him, he said, "Swamiji, how about going for a spiritual picnic, a *satsaṅga*?" "But where can we go? You drive for one hour in any direction and you reach the boundary. Where can we go?" "Swamiji, we shall go to a place five miles from here." "What is there?" "Swamiji, there is a tree there. We can all sit under the tree and have outdoor *satsaṅga* for a change." Imagine a person coming from Kerala, which is one of the greenest States, running around for miles in search of one tree. What *ānanda*, joy is there? You can make some money there but you cannot get everything, trees for example.

Wherever you go, whatever changes you bring about, the situational happiness will always be relative. Every situation has two sides—if one side is fine, the other is not. Therefore, by changing situations we cannot resolve the problem of sadness.

SEEKING

Anything you consider desirable becomes an object of seeking. There are two types of seeking in your life. First is the seeking of things that you look upon as desirable and which you do not have. Things like comforts, money, power, progeny and so on, fall in this category. You search for these things, and make efforts to gain or accomplish them with the help of knowledge, skills and resources available to you. Things appear very desirable at the moment and become *sādhya*, thing to be achieved, although, later on, you may change your views about them.

The second kind of seeking also pertains to objects that you consider desirable, but with a difference. While the first kind of seeking pertains to objects you do not have, the second kind of seeking is for the objects you have but you think you do not have. You think you do not have and therefore you seek it. It is like a man searching for his lost glasses.

This person wanted to read the newspaper on a Sunday morning. He needed his reading glasses. He opened the drawer of the desk, took out his glasses, wore them and started reading the newspaper. While he was reading, a friend came to visit him. He placed the newspaper on the side table, perched his glasses above his forehead and began talking to his friend. Half an hour later, his friend left and this man wanted to continue reading the newspaper. He picked up the paper, but could not find his reading glasses. He looked here and there. He searched in all the usual places; the glasses were not on the table, not in the drawer, and not on the floor. When he could not find them anywhere, he started shouting, "Where are my glasses?" The wife came out from the kitchen and stood there staring at him. The children also came out and dispassionately watched the drama. Finally, the youngest son could not hold it any longer and pointed at the glasses on the father's forehead. The man realised that the glasses he was searching for were with him all along.

The seeking was not because the man did not have glasses; it was because he thought he did not have glasses. He was the problem and he was the solution. He was the problem because he thought he was the non-possessor of the glasses. He was the solution because he was the possessor of the glasses. There is no physical distance between the non-possessor and the possessor of glasses. Yet there is a distance, which makes him a seeker. The distance is created by ignorance which is why you seek for what you do not have and you also seek for what you think you do not have. If you think you do not have a given thing that you consider desirable, you cannot but seek.

SEEKING IN HUMAN LIFE

If I look at my life and inquire as to what is it that I seek, I find the varieties of activities I undertake are prompted by an urge to acquire something or get rid of something. Human urges fall under three basic categories: to live, that is, to live a day longer, to gain happiness, and to acquire knowledge.

I carry out a set of activities to keep my life going, "I do not want to die today, as for tomorrow, let me see." It means there is no tomorrow; every tomorrow is today. I am alive at the present moment, and I cannot even imagine the decimation of my existence. There is a natural love to be. That I want to live is natural, universal urge, and not planted by another person. Even a newborn baby has an urge to live; it struggles to survive.

There is definitely an attempt to avoid death and, therefore, aging. But we also find people who wish to commit suicide and others who do commit. Such contradiction makes it appear as though the urge to live is not so universal; despite the urge to live, someone is ready to give up his or her life. So, I add a clause to the general rule of survival: I want to live and live happily. If I consider my entire life and conclude that the future does not hold any promise of my being happy, and sadness alone is my lot, naturally I become depressed. This wrong thinking process can prompt me to commit suicide. People commit suicide only to escape sadness. From this we understand that to live happily is as powerful an urge as the urge to live.

The third human urge is, we cannot stand ignorance. From childhood onwards, there is always an attempt to know. When you give a child a toy to play with, the first thing it does is to open it. Questions such as to why, what and how arise in the child's mind without being prompted. There is a love for gossip, for reading newspapers, magazines and so on, because nothing should go around without your knowledge. Thus, ignorance is one thing you cannot stand. You are in a great hurry and speeding in your car but if you find a group of people gathered on the sidewalk, you slow down, stick your head out and try to see what is happening there. If you want your wife to lose her sleep, just before going to bed, tell her you have an important thing to share with her, but that you will tell her the next day. She will insist you tell her just then, because she cannot stand ignorance. This is how the magazines and television serials keep your curiosity alive by cutting off the story or drama at a critical point so that you will want to read the next issue or see the next episode. We do the same thing in our talks too. So, ignorance is bliss only when it is total. If you know a little, you will want to know more.

All our activities in life are towards fulfilling these three natural urges. There are activities to stall death and old age because we have concluded that we are mortals. There are activities to make us happier than what we are. We want to get rid of unhappiness, because we have concluded that we are unhappy. We feel we are incomplete and so there is an attempt to be free from incompleteness, unhappiness. There are activities to make us more informed, more knowledgeable because we have a conclusion that we are ignorant. These three conclusions—we are mortal,

we are unhappy or incomplete, and we are ignorant—
form the basis of all human activities.

This three-fold conclusion is the problem. Vedanta
says this is an unwarranted, unjustified problem. In
the vision of Vedanta, I am just the opposite of what I
take myself to be. The notion 'I am sad' is the problem,
and it is solved only when I see the 'I' as other than
sad, as free from sadness. Vedanta says the 'I' is free
from sadness. We shall presently see how it is.

PROBLEM OF SADNESS IS CENTRED ON 'I'

If you say you are bound, then you have to be
free. If there is bondage in the 'I' sense, there alone
should be the freedom—freedom from hunger,
freedom from thirst, freedom from being bullied by
the world, freedom from being impinged upon by the
world. That freedom has to be centred on your 'I'.
It cannot be outside you, much less inside you. It has
to be you.

If the world makes you sad, then it stands to
reason that the same world must also make you happy.
You find yourself sad when you view one side of
a situation; but there is also another side, which is
as factual as this side and which makes you happy.

This is called *saṁsāra—sukhī aham*, I am happy; *duḥkhī aham*, I am unhappy. Please understand, *sukha*, happiness, is one thing and *sukhī*, happy is another. *Duḥkha*, unhappiness, pain, sorrow, is one thing and *duḥkhī*, unhappy, sorrowful, is another. It is very important to know, *duḥkha* is sorrow while *duḥkhī* is, "I am sorrowful, I am sad." Therefore, all my attempt is to remove sorrow by bringing about changes in the situations. The problem, however, is not sorrow; the problem is the notion, "*ahaṁ duḥkhī*, I am sorrowful."

Animals also experience *sukha* and *duḥkha*, pleasure and pain. They do not have the notions, '*ahaṁ sukhī*, I am happy' or '*ahaṁ duḥkhī*, I am unhappy.' A cow can be lucky if it has a master who feeds it well, and maintains it well. It is a healthy cow and it does feel some pleasure. However it does not have *sukhitva*, the notion, 'I am happy.' It does not have a complex, 'I am a superior cow, I belong to such and such family,' and so on. It does not have any of these notions or self-judgement, centred on itself. If it has crooked or ugly horns, it does not think, 'I am an ugly cow. I am stuck with these pair of horns, and I cannot remove them; others will call me a bald cow.' Cows do not have such problems. If a cow does not get food, it does feel pain and if it gets food, there definitely is some pleasure. Cows do suffer and they do experience comfort, but they do not seem to have the notions of *duḥkhitva* or *sukhitva*, of being sad or elated.

A human being, on the other hand, has a judgement centred on 'I' and it gives rise to problems. The white man wants to be white but not all that white. It is a complex and so he goes to the beach, bakes himself in the scorching heat to become less white. The black has his complex. He wants to be a little white. In India, we have our own complexes such as, "The girl is beautiful, but dark." Cows do not have such complexes. Let us take two cows of the same breed, same age and both yielding an equal quantity of milk. But there is a great difference in their selling price. Why? Because one cow has shapely horns and the other one has crooked horns. The cows themselves are not aware of that difference, and so they do not have any complex about it. It is the owner of the cows who has problems. Complexes are a human problem.

As a human being I am aware of myself as a person. In the person, I see *sukhitva* and *duḥkhitva*, the state of being happy and unhappy. So, I have complexes such as, "I am *sukhī*, happy, I am *duḥkhī*, unhappy, I am bound, I am being held down by others," and so on. These are problems. It is also a problem that I am dependent upon hundred million things for my security and happiness. The world is infinitely vast and independent of me and it has the capacity to limit me. I was born dependent upon the world, limited by it, conditioned by it. I will ever remain limited and conditioned by the world. The world definitely seems to limit me. If that is the problem, and it makes me *duḥkhī*, then the problem of *duḥkhitva* can never be solved. If my *duḥkhitva*, unhappiness arises from the world, because it limits me, I should be always sad, bound, and sorrowful.

However, in spite of my being small, unhappy, limited by the world, deprived of many things I wish to have, I do find myself occasionally a happy person. In those moments of sadness, I thought myself as sad, but now I think that I am happy. What change has taken place in the world or the self for me to become happy? The body has not changed, muchless the emotions, knowledge, memories have changed; they are all the same. The world has not changed; the job has not changed; the environment has not changed; the government has not changed; I still have any number of complaints against the community. The world very much limits me and yet I am able to laugh. When I am happy now, it means those are the moments when I look upon myself differently, entirely differently. Previously, I saw myself as *duḥkhī* and now I see myself as the one who is free from *duḥkha*. It happens even when I laugh at a simple joke.

Here is a story of a person who thought he was a cat. He was afraid of coming out of the house because there were street dogs. He thought they would chase him. He was taken to a psychiatrist who convinced him, by showing a real cat, that he was not a cat and had none of the features of a cat. By comparison with himself, the psychiatrist convinced the man that he had all the features of a human being, and he was a human being. Convinced by the psychiatrist and cured of the complex, the man came out happily. The very next day, however, he refused to go out of the house. He was again taken to the psychiatrist, who asked him,

"Aren't you convinced that you are a human being and not a cat?"

"Yes, I am convinced."

"Then why are you afraid of coming out of the house?"

The man replied, "I know I am not a cat but how do I know that the street dogs know it?" (Laughter).

You laughed at this now. What has changed in you? What problem have you solved? Your job is the same; your wife is not well; the mother-in-law has not yet left. All the problems are intact and yet you laughed.

It is true that there are problems that have to be faced factually, objectively. But the problem of sadness has nothing to do with the external world. The problem of sadness is centred on you and your notion about yourself and the world. You are the problem when you say, "I am sad." And when you laughed, what are you? You are the solution. You did not fulfil a desire nor did you solve an external problem, and yet you laughed. All that happened was you looked at yourself as you are. It means you only need to look at yourself as you are to be free from sadness.

Our scriptures say, the mind is the cause for both bondage and liberation. Mind means your notion about yourself, your conclusion, "I am this much alone." This notion, self-judgement is the problem. The solution lies in self-clarity, self knowledge. In the vision of the *upaniṣad*, the self is free. Just as in the jigsaw puzzle, when you thought the solution of the puzzle lay outside the problem, the *āpta*, the one who knows, could see the solution in the very problem. Here, in the vision of the *āpta*, the *ṛṣi*, you are the solution.

The *śāstra*'s vision, that I am the solution, seems valid enough in view of the fact that in spite of all the problems, I do see myself happy occasionally. If all these problems and notions were real, I could never give them up, and unless I give them up, I cannot be happy. The fact that I feel happy means it is possible to give up the notions about myself. Now, look at this boy who thinks that his teeth are not presentable. His teeth are not properly aligned; he has two extra teeth. He is conscious that his teeth are ugly. He deliberately avoids laughing and closes his mouth as soon as he remembers his teeth. But even this boy laughs sometimes. Do you know why? Because at that time, he is the person that he really is; he has given up the notion that he is ugly. Since that notion is not real, sometimes he catches himself laughing. It is clear, therefore, that the boy is not ugly, but he is looking upon himself wrongly. The vision of the *śāstra* is valid.

My natural longing to be free from unhappiness is further proof of the validity of the vision that the self is free and happy. There is a natural longing to be free from being unhappy. I love what is natural and I want to get rid of what is unnatural. If unhappiness, smallness, were natural to me, if they were the essential characteristics of *ātman*, the self, I could never give them up. Yet, in deep sleep and in moments of happiness, I do give up all notions that make me feel small and limited. I find myself happy when those notions are absent.

WHAT IS THE NATURE OF 'I'?

The question is, "What is the nature of 'I'? What is the dividing line between I and the world?" I feel limited by the world, which is vast and other than I. My existence is confined within certain limits. I occupy certain space and no more, and the world begins from that boundary. It is true that the world begins where the 'I' ends, and it is my conclusion that 'I' is confined to the physical body. Since my awareness of myself stops with the physical body, I conclude that I am the body; I am short, tall, fat, lean and so on. Other than the body is the entire world consisting of the five-fold sense objects.

THE LIMITATIONS OF THE PHYSICAL BODY

This physical body was not there before a given point in time. Further, during the period of its existence, it keeps changing; it is subject to aging and death. It is the nature of the body. Since I take myself to be the body, I conclude that I am subject to disease and death. I consider myself a mortal and there is always a fear of death.

The physical body has certain features, certain abilities, and it also has many limitations. It is limited in height, weight, health, and so on. Since I take myself as the physical body, these limitations become me. Time-wise, I am limited. Space-wise, I am limited; if I am here, I cannot be elsewhere at the same time. Gender-wise I am limited; if I am a male, I cannot be a female and vice versa. Again, there are limitations, colour-wise, race-wise, nation-wise... hundreds of limitations. As though this is not enough, we have added complexes like the concept of beauty. The marketing media have created notions about norms of beauty: how the eyes should be, how the eyebrows should be, what should be the colour of the skin and so on. Such notions create further complexes regarding physical appearance. As we said earlier, a cow with crooked horns does not have a complex about ugliness; it is strictly a human problem, which is an unnecessary infliction. The Lord has given a body that is alive, it is able to perform various functions. It is a gift from the Lord and we need to take it as such, without appending value judgements and complexes.

I AM A WANTING PERSON AT EVERY LEVEL

With reference to the body I am limited. Besides, I am a wanting person at every level, insecure and frightened all the time. Consequently, I add a few things to myself to become secure. However, an insecure person remains insecure. Adding or subtracting a few things does not resolve the insecurity. Neither acquisition nor renunciation can help. Acquisition becomes an endless process while giving up everything makes the person a beggar, which is an additional problem. Previously, he was begging for happiness and security, now he begs for food too.

Just as the body limits me, the sense organs and mind also limit me. Emotion-wise I am wanting; I want to remain cheerful but I cannot. How can I be happy with this kind of a body? I do not want to be sad but I become sad. Again, knowledge-wise I am wanting. I am going to be wanting all the time because there will always be something that I do not know. The more I come to know, more I become aware of all that I do not know. I find I am ignorant of many things and that makes me frustrated. Memory-wise also I am wanting. I cannot even remember what I ate yesterday. Moreover, there are things I wish to forget. For instance my brother-in-law told me something; I cannot get them out of my memory. I remember all the sad incidents and go over them again and again. In fact, they keep coming back whether[1] I like them.

---

[1] Whether or not is a common expression but the correct usage is only 'whether' without being followed by 'or not'. Whether one likes this, grammatically this is right (Author).

Thus, there is a conclusion that I am wanting in terms of time, in terms of knowledge, in terms of fullness. But the *śāstra* dismisses this conclusion.

ALL LIMITATIONS ARE OBJECTS
OF MY KNOWLEDGE

You know, you are aware of the things enumerated above, namely, the body, senses, emotions, knowledge, memories, ignorance and so on. They are all objects of your knowledge. They are there because you know them. They are not self-proving. The sun exists because you know it to exist. The wife exists because you know she exists. The physical body exists because you know it exists, that it is fat or lean, male or female, ill or healthy, and so on. If all this is known, then who is the one who knows? Obviously, you know it and others as well, although you know it much more intimately than others. It is very much an object of your knowledge, just as a sunrise or a sunset is. You know this physical body as well as other physical bodies. So, when you say, "I am tall, I am short or I am dark, fair and so on," it is just a point of view. You are looking at yourself from the standpoint of the body. All these are conclusions from the standpoint of the physical body.

If you go beyond the physical body and look at yourself, you become father, son, grandfather, husband, brother and so on. Everything you are; only the standpoints differ. From other viewpoints such as money, you have further concepts of rich, poor and so on. These are all loaded notions from different points of view. There is no harm if you know they are points of view. The problem is the points of view become the view; they become the vision of the self, the knowledge of the self.

If the physical body is an object of knowledge, if you see the body as an object, it is definitely not you, although you have a close association with your body. There is no problem even if you say, "This is my body." It is like your car. When the car gives trouble, you send it to a garage for repair; similarly, you can send your body to a hospital when it has some trouble; the only difference is that you have to go along with it. The problem arises when you identify with your body, "I am the body." You then become a mortal.

You may be a mortal from the standpoint of the body. You may be blind or deaf from the standpoint of the senses. You may be restless from the standpoint of the mind and wanting in knowledge from the standpoint of the intellect. The problem is you are mortal, restless, ignorant, sinner and so on. There are so many complexes that arise when you look at yourself from different standpoints. But from the standpoint of 'I' that is aware of the body, senses, emotions, knowledge, memories, ignorance, what are you? Who are you? Look at yourself from the standpoint of 'I'. What is that 'I'? When you look at it, you can only say, I am a conscious being, a person who is aware. Do you require a proof? I ask you,

"What is this?"

"A flower."

"How do you know?"

"Because I see."

So you know things that are existent and non-existent. Now I ask you,

"Do you exist or not?"

"I have no doubt that I exist."

"How do you know you exist?"

You exist because everything else requires proof for its existence whereas you require no proof. The existence of everything is proven because you exist. If you needed proof of your existence, you would have no knowledge. 'I' is self-evident, simple consciousness.

Consciousness has no form. When you see my hand, the hand is within your consciousness. Hand has a form but consciousness has no form. So, *caitanya*, consciousness, is *aparicchinna*, limitless—limitless in terms of form, space and time. It is the meaning of 'I'. The physical body is in time, therefore it is mortal; it comes and goes. But when time is, consciousness is. When time goes, consciousness still is. You are conscious of time. Time is an object of your consciousness. Time is something that can disappear. There is no time between two thoughts; there is no time when you are in ecstasy; there is no time when you are asleep. You are conscious of time. You are also conscious of space and things in space and time. Everything exists in time and space, and time and space exist in consciousness. Everything is in consciousness. The known, *vidita* and the unknown, *avidita*, both are in consciousness.

I find my body imperfect, my mind inadequate, but the problem is, I think I am imperfect and inadequate, since I identify with the body and mind.

HAPPINESS IS IN SPITE OF UNFULFILLED DESIRES

When I look back at my life, as far as I can remember, there was not a single day when I was totally free from desires, when I was totally free from being a wanting person, when all my desires were fulfilled. On any given day, I find that I have some desires unfulfilled. As a child, when I wanted to eat one more candy, it was 'no.' I did not want to go to school, again it was 'no.' I did not want to play, but I had to go. When I wanted to play, then it was 'no.' So as a child, I was a wanting person, as a young man, a wanting person, unmarried, a wanting person, married, a wanting person, as an old person, I continue to be a wanting person. My complaint is nobody listens to me, nobody behaves properly and so on.

Logically, it is impossible for you to be happy even for a moment because all the time, you are wanting. At any given time, you have any number of desires that are not fulfilled or cannot be fulfilled. There is always a situation when you have things that you do not want, or you do not have things that you want. Yet occasionally you are happy. It is your experience. You got something you wanted, you are happy. You hear a joke, you are happy. You solve a problem and you are happy. You are happy because someone said, "You are wonderful." Although logically it is impossible for you to be happy, you are able to see it is possible for you to be happy. If these moments are not there, you will commit suicide. These moments keep life going. However, you gather these moments not by fulfilling all your desires; you gather them in spite of desires. The world does not disappear when you are happy; it is very much there. Whatever you confront is the world for you. The world can be the sky, the stars, any sense object, or anything you confront at a given time. When you interact with your child, the child is the world for you.

SEEKER-SOUGHT DIVISION IS RESOLVED WHEN YOU RECOGNISE YOURSELF AS THE WHOLE

When I am happy, at that moment, the world is, the senses are, the mind is and I am very much present. My situations have not changed and complaints have not gone away. The problems have not been solved; the roof is leaking, the house needs painting, but I am still happy. What does it mean? It only means, at any moment when I am happy, I am not a seeker; the conclusion, 'I am wanting,' is not there.

With reference to the world, I am always a seeker. I want humanity to be different. I want the government to be different. I want people who are near and dear, to be different. Thus, with reference to any thing, be it money-wise, power-wise, name-wise, influence-wise, friendship-wise, I am a wanting person, a seeker. Even with reference to role-playing, I am a seeker, as a daughter-in-law, as a mother-in-law, as a father, mother, son, and so on. I am always a wanting person. I want the world that I relate to be different. I am constantly a seeker.

What happens in a moment of joy? I cease to be a seeker. There is no division between the world and me. The seeker-sought division disappears at that moment. There is no judgement about the self, how lonely I am; how useless I am; how worthless I am; how ugly I am and so on. Such conclusions are completely forgotten; I have forgotten my height, my weight. Suddenly I become one with the world. Both the world and I become complete, whole. It is called *pūrṇa*. What I confront is *pūrṇa*, and I, who confronts the world, am also *pūrṇa*. There is no *bheda*, division between I and the world. I become *pūrṇa*, whole, complete. I am happy because I am the whole. That is, I am consciousness, fullness in spite of the body, senses, mind, and world.

We never say the world is *duḥkha*, sorrowful; we say *saṃsāra* is *duḥkha*. *Saṃsāra* is a notion, born of ignorance of what I am, thinking I am a seeker, I am lacking and so on. In moments of happiness, this notion is absent; there is no seeker-sought duality, and there is fullness. That fullness is you.

Fullness does not belong to the world. Fullness is not a particular object. Your body is not fullness, your mind is not fullness; all these have their limitations. The 'I' is fullness. In the moment of fullness you forget yourself. Which self? The self that has the notion, 'I am so and so,' that feels useless, frustrated, that self is forgotten; the *ahaṅkāra* is forgotten, and at that moment you are happy, which is your true nature.

You experience the self that is happiness but you do not know. Since there is experience, you want to do the same thing again, and so what do you do? You make arrangements. You arrange the world. You manipulate so that the same experience comes to you again. However, the same experience never repeats. You go on manipulating the world but it does not work. Whenever they happen, in moments of joy, you are yourself. You do not have any wish; you do not want anything to change.

THE 'I-NOTION' IS THE PROBLEM

The whole problem is the 'I–notion,' the notion, 'I am unhappy.' Therefore, the solution is knowledge that 'I am happiness.' In fact, the solution lies in the unhappiness itself. The person who is unhappy, has the solution just as the solution is in the very jigsaw puzzle. Once the pieces fall in their place, the problem is solved; it is no longer a puzzle. Similarly, the world that is a threat to me has to fall in its place in terms of the reality it has and I have to fall in my place in terms of the reality I am. When this happens, I find there is only solution; there is no problem at all. All that remains are only problems such as hunger, thirst and so on, which are factual topical problems. The problem of human life is entirely different; it is not removing sorrow, it is removing the notion, 'I am sorrowful.' *Duḥkha*, pain, is not the problem, 'I am sad, I am in pain,' is the problem. Bondage is not the problem; 'I am bound' is the problem. I am the problem, and the solution lies within me. I need to seek it within myself.

YOU ARE THE SOLUTION

Suppose you are in a beautiful place, the luxury of nature all around, mountains, and greenery. The place is clean and the people are good. Everything is beautiful and you find yourself happy. Do you know why?

It is because you do not want the mountain to be different; you do not want the colour of the sky to be different; you do not want the river to be different; you do not want the stones around you to be different; you do not want your body to be different. In fact, you just are, are you not? You accept yourself totally because you find yourself acceptable. The 'I' is but consciousness. It is already full, limitless. You experience it whenever you are happy. Whether it is *viṣayānanda*, joy coming from sense-objects, or *yogānanda*, joy coming from *yoga*, or *vidyānanda*, joy coming from knowledge, it is yourself alone that you experience, you that is fullness. You are limitless because consciousness is limitless, *ananta*, which is the same as *ānanda*.

It is the limitlessness, *ānanda*, the fullness that I am, that I experience in different degrees. I am limitless time-wise and so I am not mortal. I am limitless space-wise and so I am not incomplete. I am consciousness that illumines both knowledge and ignorance, and so I am neither knowledgeable nor ignorant, to be limited by them. I am already what I want to be, free from death, incompleteness and ignorance. I am the very solution to my problem.

So, you are the problem, you are the solution. It is an insight into you. It makes one fact very clear.

You need to know you are the solution, you are consciousness, fullness. We do not say you will become something. We say you are everything, and to know that you need clarity. The problem is centred on 'I' and the solution is centred on that very 'I,' the reality of which is entirely different from what you take it to be. Therefore, the solution lies in the very problem; it is not outside the problem.

The human problem is that regardless of what you do, you find yourself a wanting person. It is because you cannot give up the conclusion 'I am wanting.' It can only be forgotten. So, what people, generally try to do is to forget themselves. They go for holidays, and perhaps go as far as Hawaii, spending a lot of money and time to forget themselves, which is what happens when you are happy. There are a lot of things you can accomplish to improve the quality of life, to make your life better than what it is. But for being happy, and free from being unhappy, you are the problem, you are the solution. 'I am unhappy' is the problem; 'I am free from unhappiness' is the solution. It is not delusion; it is reality, the reality to which you need to become alive.

Oṁ tat sat

BOOKS BY SWAMI DAYANANDA SARASWATI

Public Talk Series :
1. Living Intelligently
2. Successful Living
3. Need for Cognitive Change
4. Discovering Love
5. The Value of Values
6. Vedic View and Way of Life

Upaniṣad Series :
7. Muṇḍakopaniṣad
8. Kenopaniṣad

Prakaraṇa Series :
9. Tattvabodhaḥ

Text Translation Series :
10. Śrīmad Bhagavad Gītā
    (Text with roman transliteration and English translation)
11. Śrī Rudram
    (Text in Sanskrit with transliteration, word-to-word and verse meaning along with an elaborate commentary in English)

Stotra Series :
12. Dīpārādhanā
13. Prayer Guide
    (With explanations of several Mantras, Stotras, Kirtans and Religious Festivals)

Moments with Oneself Series :

Bhagavad Gītā

Meditation Series :

Essays :

Exploring Vedanta Series : (*vākyavicāra*)

Books translated in other languages and in English based on Swami Dayananda Saraswati's Original Exposition

Tamil

Distributed in India & worldwide by
MOTILAL BANARSIDASS - NEW DELHI
Tel : 011 - 2385 8335 / 2385 1985 / 2385 2747

Also available at :

ARSHA VIDYA RESEARCH
AND PUBLICATION TRUST
32 / 4 Sir Desika Road
Mylapore Chennai 600 004
Telefax : 044 - 2499 7131
Email : avrandpc@gmail.com
Website : www.avrpt.com

ARSHA VIDYA GURUKULAM
Anaikatti P.O.
Coimbatore 641 108
Ph : 0422 - 2657001
Fax : 0422 - 2657002
Email : office@arshavidya.in
Website : www.arshavidya.in

ARSHA VIDYA GURUKULAM
P.O.Box 1059. Pennsylvania
PA 18353, USA
Ph : 001 -570 -992 -2339
Email : avp@epix.net
Website : www.arshavidya.org

SWAMI DAYANANDA ASHRAM
Purani Jhadi, P.B.No. 30
Rishikesh, Uttaranchal 249 201
Telefax: 0135 - 2430769
Email : ashrambookstore@yahoo.com
Website : www.dayananda.org

Other leading Book Stores:

Chennai:	044
Motilal Banarsidass	2498 2315
Giri Trading	2495 1966
Higginbothams	2851 3519
Pustak Bharati	2461 1345
Theosophical Publishing House	2446 6613 / 2491 1338
The Odessey	43910300

Bengaluru:	**080**
Gangarams	2558 1617 / 2558 1618
Sapna Book House	4011 4455 / 4045 5999
Strand Bookstall	2558 2222, 2558 0000
Vedanta Book House	2650 7590

Coimbatore:	**0422**
Guru Smruti	9486773793
Giri Trading	2541523

Trivandrum:	**0471**
Prabhus Bookhouse	2478397 / 2473496

Kozhikode:	**0471**
Ganga Bookhouse	6521262

Mumbai:	**022**
Chetana Bookhouse	2285 1243 / 2285 3412
Strand Bookstall	2266 1994 / 2266 1719 / 2261 4613
Giri Trading	2414 3140